Raspberry Pi 2

(101 Beginners Guide)

The Definitive Step by Step guide for what you need to know to get started

Table of Contents

Introduction to Raspberry Pi 2

Chapter 1: Some History of the Raspberry Pi 2

Chapter 2: Raspberry Pi 2 Capabilities

Chapter 3: Connecting and Booting up your Raspberry Pi 2

Chapter 4: Installing an operating System

Chapter 5: Common Uses for Raspberry Pi 2

Chapter 6: Fantastic Raspberry Pi 2 Projects

Chapter 7: Common Programming Languages used with Pi 2

Chapter 8: Creating Games with the Raspberry Pi 2

Chapter 9: Getting Creative with your Pi 2 **(Limited time BONUS Chapter)**

Chapter 10: Top Success tips when working with a Pi 2

Chapter 11: Raspberry Pi Events, Communities & Meetups

Chapter 12: Fantastic Online Resources for the Raspberry Pi 2

Conclusion

Introduction to Raspberry Pi 2

Are you a person who always likes to know about the latest about advances in technology? Are you a teacher who is frustrated with the lack of resources available to teach computer science and information technology? Perhaps you are someone who has heard of the Raspberry Pi 2 and is just curious as to what it is exactly.

This book will tell you everything that you need to know about the Raspberry Pi 2. It is packed with the specifications of the microcomputer, a step by step guide on how to set it up, tips and tricks for using it, and tons of resources. With this valuable guide, you will go from knowing nothing at all about what you can do with a Raspberry Pi to knowing everything that there is to be done with the Pi.

It will also tell you the main differences between the Raspberry Pi and the Raspberry Pi 2. There is a lot of comparison and contrast so that even if it is not your first time dealing with the Pi, and you just want to know what the big deal is about version 2, you will be able to find out.

The Pi 2 was created in order to offer a greater performance quality than its predecessors, and that it does. It can run unique software, which means more opportunities for programming and exploring. It also can run faster than the original Pi, due to its more powerful CPU. This tool was intended to be used in the classroom in order teach programming, and there is no doubt that it will excel at just that.

The reason that this book was written was to make sure that you get the maximum advantages when it comes to your Raspberry Pi 2 experience. There is no reason why you should grope in the dark, attempting to understand the ins and outs of the device when you could be already creating amazing gadgets and programs.

With this veritable goldmine of information at your fingertips, there is no way that you will not be blown away by this amazing device and all that it can do. Soon, you will be learning programming and making your own projects, as well.

So, what are you waiting for? Start your Raspberry Pi 2 experience now by reading on to the next chapter.

Chapter 1: Some History of the Raspberry Pi 2

The Raspberry Pi 2 is the latest generation of the Raspberry Pi microcomputer. The original Raspberry Pi was invented by the Raspberry Pi Foundation, a charity that was founded in 2009. The aim of the Raspberry Pi was to reinvent the teaching and learning of basic computer skills. Four computer science engineers, Eben Upton, Rob Mullins, JAck Land and Alan Mycroft, noted that students were no longer applying to the Computer Science major in universities and that those who did, did not have all of the skills that they should. So began the Raspberry Pi.

The problem that was causing students to lose interest in computer science related majors was the absence of adequate computer education in schools, which was an effect of the lack of available resources. Therefore, the answer was a computer that was small and also affordable. The Raspberry Pi is a single board computer that is no bigger than a credit card, running the Broadcom BCM2835 system on a chip. There are four different models of the Raspberry Pi.

A Brief Introduction to the Raspberry Pi 2

The Raspberry Pi 2 is the first version of the Raspberry Pi to run BCM2836, rather than BCM2835. On its website, the Raspberry Pi Foundation states that they have spent a lot of resources getting the most that they could get out of the original model's Broadcom BCM2835 processor and its 700 megahertz ARM11 CPU. They have created optimized versions of several open-source libraries and applications, with the goal of transforming the Raspberry Pi into the most stable single board computer in the world.

However, they reached a point where they needed more memory and a higher performing central processing unit, but they did not want to waste all of their effort in the platform or ruin all of the projects and tutorials online that were only compatible with the current Raspberry Pi models. It was around this time the Broadcom introduced a new system-on-chip: BCM2836. This was perfect because it had all of the features of the BCM2835, with the exception of replacing the old central processing unit with a 900 megahertz quad-core ARM Cortex-A7 complex.

Educational Goals for the Raspberry Pi 2

As mentioned, the Raspberry Pi Foundation's focus is the development of computer science education for students and teachers across the globe. The Raspberry Pi 2 will certainly further this aim, with its increased performance and great value. It can be bought for only US$35. Using this resources, primary school students will be able to learn basic computer programming and eventually use the Pi 2 for a wide range of technological projects and experiments, increasing their knowledge of computer science and engineering and increasing the number of students who enter secondary and tertiary education with the intent of becoming a computer scientist or an engineer.

Chapter 2: Raspberry Pi 2 Capabilities

The Raspberry Pi 2 has a unique set of capabilities as compared to its predecessors. It runs Broadcom BCM 2836, whereas the earlier models of the Raspberry Pi run BCM2835. It also does not have the 700 megahertz single-core ARM1176JZF-S central processing unit that the others have. Rather, it runs using a 900 megahertz quad-core ARM Cortex-A7 CPU. It has 1 gigabyte of on board memory and four USB ports, like the Raspberry Pi Model B+.

It shares the same video input features as the other models, which is a 15-pin MIPI camera inerfaces connecter, which can be used with the Raspberry Pi camera or Raspberry Pi NoIR camera. It has fourteen HDMI resolutions for video output from 640x350 to 1920x1200 and different PAL and NTSC standards. It also has composite video output through a 3.5 mm TRRS jack, which is shared with audio output. It has two boards for audio inputs and gives analog audio outputs through a 3.5 mm phone jack. Digital audio output are delivered through HDMI.

For extended storage, there is a microSD slot, and it has on board Ethernet capabilities with the use of a 10/100 megabit per second Ethernet USB adapter. There are seventeen general purpose input/output(GPIO) pins with HAT ID bus and it has a power rating of four Watts. The Raspberry Pi 2 is powered using a microUSB or GPIO header and measures 85.60 mm x 56.5 mm in size, weighing 45 grams.

The Raspberry Pi 2, Compared to Earlier Models

Model A

In comparison, the Model A, the most basic and original version of the Raspberry Pi, weighs the same, has the same measurements, and is powered using the same source. However, its power ratings are only 2.5 watts, it only has eight GPIO pins with add-ons that can also be used as GPIO, such as UART and SPI bus with two chip selects.

The Raspberry Pi Model A does not have any on board Internat capabilities and for storage, it is compatible with an SD, MMC or SDIO card. For video output, it offers the same range of resolutions as the Pi 2, but for composite video it uses an RCA jack. This model only has one USB port, which is directly connected to the BCM2835 chip, and only has 256 megabytes of random access memory. It is sold for US$25.

Model A+

The model A+ is even cheaper than the model A at US$20, and it is the smallest in size out of all of the models. Besides this, it only has a few differences compared to the model a, such as video outputs being shared with the audio outputs through a TRRS jack, like the Raspberry Pi 2. Other things that Model A+ has in common with the Raspberry Pi 2 are the low level-peripherals specifications (seventeen GPIO and HAT ID bus), and the use of a microSD slot for added memory.

Model B

The Model B is sold at the same price as the Pi 2, but has only 512 megabytes of system memory. It also only has two USB ports. It outputs composite video through an RCA jack, like the Model A and uses a and SD/MMC/SDIO card slot for storage extension, also like the Model A. Like the Pi 2, this model is Ethernet capable, even though it has the same amount of GPIO pins and low-level peripheral specifications as the model A. The Raspberry Pi 2 and the Raspberry Pi Model B are the same size and weight.

Model B+

The Pi 2 and the Model B+ share almost all of their specs. the only exceptions are the amount of system storage on the B+, which is 512 megabytes, and the central processing unit, which is the same as that of Models A, A+ and B.

Chapter 3: Connecting and Booting Up Your Raspberry Pi 2

Getting started with your Raspberry Pi 2 and setting it up for use is not a complicated process at all. You just need to follow a few simple steps, and your Raspberry Pi 2 will be ready to use in no time at all.

Before You Begin

Before you connect your Raspberry Pi and Boot it up, there are few items you will need to gather. One very important thing that you will need is a microSD card. This is how you will install your operating system, which you will need in order to run your Raspberry Pi 2. You can either buy a microSD card with an operating system pre-installed or buy an empty microSD card and download an operating system onto it. NOOBS and Raspbian are ideal starter operating systems, both of which you can download from the foundation's website. For the Raspberry Pi 2, you will need to have an updated version of NOOBS or Raspbian with the ARMv7 kernel and modules.

The next thing that you will need are display cables in order to connect the Pi 2 to a display monitor or TV and an Ethernet cable for Internet access. Ideally, you should use a monitor that has HDMI input, but you can use devices with other connections as long a you use an HDMI adapter to connect to the Raspberry Pi 2. If you are not using an HDMI connection, you will want speaker or headphones with a 3.5 mm jack in order to hear sound. You will also need a keyboard and mouse, of course. A standard USB keyboard and mouse will do. Finally, you will need a 5V micro USB cord to supply power for your device.

Connecting and Booting Your Pi 2

After you are sure that you have all of the items that you need, you can start to connect your Pi 2. Here are your step by step instructions for putting all of the pieces together to make your raspberry Pi 2 run.

Step 1: Insert your microSD card into the appropriate slot on your Raspberry Pi 2.

Step 2: Plug your keyboard and mouse into their respective USB slots.

Step 3: Turn your display monitor or TV on, and select the proper input.

Step 4: Use your display cable to connect your Raspberry Pi 2 to the display monitor.

Step 5: Plug the Ethernet cable into your Raspberry Pi 2 in order to connect it to the Internet.

Step 6: Connect your Raspberry Pi 2 to the power supply using your microUSB cable. This will turn on your Raspberry Pi and it will boot.

Step 7: Since this is the first time that you are booting your Raspberry Pi 2, you will need to select your operating system and configure it. Depending on the operating system that you are using to begin with (NOOBS or Raspbian), you can follow a guide available on the Raspberry Foundation Website in order to complete this step.

Logging In to Your Pi 2

You will be prompted to log in once your Raspberry Pi 2 has completely booted. The default username is 'pi' and the password is 'raspberry'. Do not be alarmed if you do not see any writing when you type in the password, as this is a security feature of the operating system. Once you have logged in, you will see a command line prompt that says 'pi@raspberrypi~$'. To load the user interface, simply type 'startx' and press *Enter*.

These steps will get your started on the road to exploring the amazing things that you can do with your Raspberry Pi 2.

Chapter 4: Installing an Operating System

The increased memory and power of the Raspberry Pi 2 in comparison to the previous models of the Pi has made it possible to run many operating systems that were not able to run on the original Raspberry Pi. Of course, the Pi 2 also runs many updated versions of the more popular systems for the Raspberry Pi. Some operating systems that you can still run with the Raspberry Pi 2, include NOOBS, Raspbian, OpenELEC, Snappy Ubuntu Core and Debian Jessie.

Some operating systems that you can use on the Pi 2 that you could not have used on the original Pi are OSMC (an updated version of Raspbmc, which cannot work with the Pi 2), Ubuntu 14.10 with LXDE and Fedora 21. Other systems are in the process of creating updates that will make them compatible with the Pi 2, like RetroPie and Windows 10 IoT version.

Common Operating Systems Used with the Raspberry Pi 2

In this chapter, we will discuss some of the pros and cons of a few of the operating systems that can be run on the Raspberry Pi 2, focusing on those that were not available for the Raspberry Pi.

Fedora 21

First generation models of the Raspberry Pi had to use a customized version of the Fedora operating system, called Pidora, which was developed specifically for use with the Pi. The Raspberry Pi 2, however can run the official operating system. This operating system is built with the ability to incorporate new technology over the course of a longer period of time than most operating systems.

While it has many benefits, this can be a challenging operating system to navigate, because in order to do so, you need to be comfortable dealing with terminal commands in Linux. The installation process is also a bit challenging, as you have to begin by installing the latest version of the Raspbian OS. You can take a look at the process yourself, and learn more about this operating system at https://getfedora.org/

Ubuntu 14.10 with LXDE

While the Raspberry Pi 2 can already run Snappy Ubuntu Core, this version of Ubuntu was specifically developed for it. It is designed to make the best use of all of the features that come with Pi 2's ARMv7 processor. Users say that the web browser on the operating system is at least as responsive as that on the Raspbian operating system, the most popular system for the Pi and Pi 2.

There are actually no significant differences between this and the Raspbian operating system. However, it is worth noting, that it may not have all of the optimized features that Raspbian comes pre-installed with in order to make the Pi 2 the perfect learning tool, and to create ease of use for beginning Pi 2 users. To learn more about this operating system, go to http://releases.ubuntu.com/14.10/

OSMC

As mentioned before, OSMC (Open Source Media Center) is the successor to Raspbmc, which is not compatible with the Raspberry Pi 2. This operating system is optimal for executing any media related projects at all. This can include watching TV using a tuner, playing videos from Netflix, Hulu and Amazon and playing videos or music. It is also extremely simple to install, installing and running after just a few prompts about things such as language. Another great thing about this operating system is that there are several add-ons that have been developed by users which are available for download.

For right now, this operating system is still in its early stages of development, so there is some continuing work to be done in order to improve its performance and its stability in terms of the Raspberry Pi 2. Some users have complained about the operation of the keyboard and the mouse with this operating system. Also, while music stored on USB plays well, there is a lag in some functions, such as the audio playback controller appearing on the screen. You can read more about OSMC at https://osmc.tv/

Chapter 5: Common Uses for the Raspberry Pi 2

With the Raspberry Pi 2's increased memory and power, there are a brand new world of possibilities for things that can be done with it. Some of the tutorials that Raspberry Pi users have created may be an inspiration to many who own the Pi 2, and likely, you can create even better versions of these projects, due to the added features on this version of the device.

Just like its predecessors, the Raspberry Pi 2 is a great tool for children to learn about computer hardware, software and programming. It is also great for adults who are interested in exploring the world of computer science. It is used in classrooms and homes around the world to expand knowledge about open-source and software coding. It can help to develop problem solving skills in young students and even people with almost no computer coding background knowledge will be able to do a lot with this computer.

Of course, the most common use for the Pi is the obvious, a cheap and super simple desktop computer. However, you can also use it as a substitute Smart TV, using OSMC. With a few easy steps, and downloading a remote control app on your smart phone, you will be able to watch videos on YouTube, and even stream videos from your phone. You can also play videos on your hard drive because the Pi 2 can playback full screen 1080 pixel video.

Some people use the Pi 2 as a game console, to make a printer and even automatic dog feeders. One of the most exciting things that can be done with the Pi 2 is using it to create and control a robotic element. Users have created robots out of Legos, and others that can do things like dye Easter eggs.

The Pi is also commonly used to power projects such as home security cameras, automation systems and other technologically advanced ways to make life much easier. Some users even put their Raspberry Pi 2 to use as a personal web server, in which they save documents or media, or operate web based games like Minecraft.

The possibilities for your Raspberry Pi 2 are endless indeed. With a bit of research, you can make it into anything.

Chapter 6: Fantastic Raspberry Pi 2 Projects

There are a lot of amazing things that you can do with your Raspberry Pi 2, in fact the the options may seem endless. Here are a few fantastic things that can be done with your Pi 2, with links to instructables and tutorials on how to do them.

Use the Raspberry Pi 2 as a NAS drive

One thing that you can do with your Pi 2 is use it as network attached storage drive by using portable drives. This is a great use for your device if you are a person who needs a lot of backup storage space, or if you just want to expand the extent of your system memory. You can complete this project in a few simple steps. Learn more in this video:

https://www.youtube.com/watch?v=T5eKBfstpI0

Server Room Environmental Monitor

The Raspberry Pi 2 can also be used as an environmental monitoring system. The project described at http://www.bigi.com/rjb/Projects/ServerRoomEnvironmentals/ uses the Pi to support 44 temperature sensors, which also read humidity and light levels. The Pi then communicates with a PCB, which does the work of collecting environmental data.

Raspberry Pi Powered Cat Feeder

One Pi user found a solution to the problem of traveling without pets. When he was scheduled to go on a weekend trip with his girlfriend who was going to leave her two cats behind, he decided to design an automated cat feeder for them, rather than leaving a a large bowl of cat food out, as most owners do. This project is completed and it works well, so if you are a pet owner, it will definitely be of interest to you. To make one of your own, go to http://www.tcmaker.org/blog/2013/03/raspberry-pi-powered-cat-feeder/

Raspberry Pi Powered EggBot

This robot is built to color eggs, and has a Raspberry Pi embedded within it to operate it. This is a great tool for teaching younger students about robotics, while honoring the theme of Easter. It is also effective to use at home, if you are the kind of person who likes to plan Easter egg hunts. Check this project out at http://www.instructables.com/id/How-to-Embed-a-Raspberry-Pi-into-your-eggbot/?ALLSTEPS

Home Automation

This project creates a home automation system which is convenient and easy to build. It uses Arduino, and will solve any issues that you may have regarding help, friends or family arriving at your house when you are not there. This gadget will only cost you about ninety dollars to make, and you can program it to either send notifications to your phone or email address. Find out how to use your Raspberry Pi 2 for this convenient project at https://speakerdeck.com/pyconslides/whos-there-home-automation-with-arduino-and-raspberrypi-by-rupa-dachere

"Chicago Faces"

A Pi user living in Chicago has invented an artistic use for the Raspberry Pi. "Chicago Faces" is a guerrilla art composition which photographs the faces of strangers using open source hardware and software. The Raspberry Pi itself has a street camera embedded in it, which runs a facial recognition algorithm. Once the camera-computer combination discovers a face, it takes a picture which is automatically uploaded to Twitter and tweeted via the project's Twitter account. Learn more about this project and see how you might be able to create one for your own area at http://danbertner.wordpress.com/work/chicagofaces/

Home Alarm Plus

Another invaluable project for home management is this open source home alarm monitoring system. It functions using the Raspberry Pi, Netduino Plus, ATTiny 85 and a normal home alarm system. The way the system works is by sending a notification to the home owner's phone when an area or sensor has been compromised. The notification is accompanied by an email that describes the details of the compromised zone. Check this project out, and have it set up in no time! http://homealarmpluspi.blogspot.com/2013/04/blog-post.html

Piano "Teacher"

Some musicians, who are also Pi enthusiasts, were able to create a system that makes it faster and more simple to learn chords. The Easy as Pi Piano System actually functions as an electronic piano teacher. It teaches the user how to play the chords to their favorite songs, and lasers guide them to play the correct keys. On the display monitor, users see the correct finger placements, the name of the chord, and lyrics to the song. Learn how to enhance your piano playing experience, or learn to play if you don't know how by watching the video about this project. http://www.youtube.com/watch?v=Y1Mh4tDgZPk&feature=youtu.be

BrickPi

BrickPi converts the Raspberry Pi into a robot. The project consists of a board and case which connect LEGO Mindstorms sensors, motors and parts with the Raspberry Pi in order to turn it into a robot. A 9V battery is used as a power source, which powers the motors, sensors and the Raspberry Pi, which will allow your robot a full range of motion, as the Pi will not have to be connected to a power source with the microUSB cable. This is a fun project for students and you can find the details on http://www.dexterindustries.com/BrickPi/introduction/

KA-Pi

For teachers, this project is definitely a must-try. This is an extremely simple educational set up for the Raspberry Pi. The Pi is configured to deliver pre-loaded Khan Academy offline content into your classroom - just plug and play. The website features more than two thousand video lectures on Math and Science, and it works great for a classroom where there is no Internet connection available. Just download the content at http://pi.mujica.org/ transfer it to a 16 GB SD card and insert the card into your Pi.

Electric Vehicle Charging Station

If you are concerned about the welfare of the environment, and have decided to drive a low emitting, hybrid or fully electric vehicle, this project is worth your while. It is not very hard to do, and it can be built and stationed at a public community center, such as a college campus or school so that drivers can charge their vehicles conveniently, away from home. One user built one that would use the existing ID cards for the university campus. Take a look: http://blog.ovccorp.com/

Hydroponic Automation Platform Initiative (HAPI)

This project is changing the world of agriculture and food production by collaborating with open source technology, such as Arduino, to create automatic control of food production sites. This device monitors the lighting, nutrient and PH levels, pumps, tank flushes, data logging and interfaces at a food production site. It also creates reports and documentation of collected data. Learn more about this groundbreaking technology at http://hapihq.com/

Chapter 7: Common Programming Languages Used with Pi 2

There are basically an endless amount of options when it comes to what programming language you will choose to use with your Raspberry Pi 2. Just like the Raspberry Pi, it is very versatile and you can use just about any language that you would want to use. Ultimately, the programming language that you decide on will depend on what you would like to do with your Pi.

Python is the most popular programming language, as it is recommended for beginners. Scratch is popular in schools, because it is simple and very effective for teaching younger students the basics of computer programming. You can also use C++, Erlang, Perl, C programming language, Java, JQuery, JavaScript, and HTML5. In this chapter, we will discuss a few of the most popular programming languages for the Raspberry Pi 2 in detail as well as their pros and cons in terms of the Pi.

Python

Python is the most popular programming language for use with the Raspberry Pi 2. It is simple and especially popular in academic settings for this reason. The Raspberry Pi Foundation recommends it for users who are just getting started in the programming world. This is due to its versatility, and productivity, as wells as the fact that this language uses less wording than other codes.

Earlier versions of Python designed to use with Pi were a bit slow, due to the fact that it was an interpreted language. However, the newest version are being optimized to run at the same speed as the other programming languages. If you want to develop applications for mobile phones, this is not the best language to learn because it is not available for mobile platforms. Besides some minor design limitations, this is a great and flexible programming language for any Raspberry Pi 2 owner to use.

C Programming Language

C programming language is one of the most popular programming languages used across the globe in general. It has been used to write everything from entire operating systems, to simple programming languages. In fact, Linux, which is one of the operating systems that runs the Raspberry Pi 2, is mostly written with C. The design for this programming language has been influential in the development of many others, including Python. It has even been extended into a programming language called objective C, which is the language used for writing iPhone and iPad applications.

All of this being said, it comes as no surprise that C is a popular choice for programming on the Raspberry Pi 2. The Raspberry Pi was quite slow for an integrated developing environment, or using a combination of Linux and another programming language together for ease of use. However, the increase power and speed of the Pi 2 has made doing this much easier, as it may be quite limiting for your purposes to program only using the Linux command line.

Scratch

Scratch is the best entry-level programming language for teaching young students to learn programming. It comes already installed with the Raspbian operating system. The most common use for Scratch on the Raspberry Pi 2 is creating simple games and animation. Users love it because it introduces beginners to many of the fundamental concepts of programming while also being easy to use. If you have never programmed before, it is an essential skill for you to learn in order to make the most of your Pi 2. This is the perfect language to begin your journey with.

What makes Scratch so easy is that it breaks down the aspects of learning code. In order to code, you need to know the underlying logic that makes the program function in addition to the actual code. Scratch strips the code away so that you can get to understand the logic part of it. This is a good starting point for new learners, and you can choose to incorporate the code as you become more advanced.

Chapter 8: Creating Games with the Raspberry Pi 2

Of course, one of the best ways to enjoy your Raspberry Pi 2 is by using it to create and enjoy your own games. The Pi 2 is quite versatile when it comes to this, as you can learn to recreate your favorite games and even create custom games using your own original ideas. While the Pi 2 does not support emulator operating system RetroPie as yet, you can still run an emulator on one of the many operating systems that it does support in order to turn your device into a retro gaming powerhouse.

Those Pi users who have not learned enough about programming to design their own games using the Pi 2 and programming languages like Scratch or Python, can still enjoy playing games by downloading games available in the Raspberry Pi Store. In order to make it easier for users to begin designing their own games, some programming languages, like Python feature add-ons which are developed specifically to guide beginners through the process of programming a game.

While creating and playing computer games with the Raspberry Pi 2 is the obvious thing to do, there are other types of games that can be designed with this microcomputer. One user designed a NERF-dart shooting robot with the Pi. If you love NERF, you can surprise your friends with a sneak attack once you design this robot.

Another way for you to enjoy games with your Raspberry Pi 2, is by using it to power a handheld game console. You can create replicas of your favorite consoles like the Game Boy Pocket, or the Game Boy Advanced and play vintage games on it. Parents and educators have also found it effective to use the Pi 2 as a Minecraft Machine, as Minecraft is a game that many children enjoy playing.

Game Project Tutorials

Raspberry Jolt

This is a Raspberry Pi powered robot that shoots NERF darts. The robot has WiFi control and remote video recording. Besides the Pi, its other components are a server with a linear conversion kit and a NERF gun positioned on top of a first generation Romo by Romotive. Learn how to create this awesome game at http://jordanbalagot.com/blog/2013/02/26/raspberry-jolt-my-mini-nerf-gun-robot/?autoplay=false

Handheld Raspberry Pi 2 Game Console

This project can turn your Pi 2 into one of your favorite game consoles from the nineties. It creates a Raspberry Pi operated Game Boy Pocket. While the tutorial features the Raspberry Pi, this project can also be completed using the Pi 2. http://lifehacker.com/how-to-build-a-handheld-raspberry-pi-powered-game-cons-1663675758

Making Your Own Game on Raspberry Pi 2

If you are the parent or teacher of children who like to create things, or you are an adult who likes to express you own creativity, you will find this tutorial fun. It will show you how to use Python programming to create your very own game for Raspberry Pi. Take a look at http://www.linuxuser.co.uk/tutorials/make-a-game-on-raspberry-pi

Dedicated Minecraft Machine

You can use your Raspberry Pi 2 as an around the clock server for your Minecraft game. This is a great way to enjoy your Minecraft experience to the max. You can let friends and family build in your would by leaving your server on 24/7 and increase control over your multiplayer game much better than you can using a public server. Learn how to do this at http://www.howtogeek.com/173044/how-to-run-low-cost-minecraft-on-a-raspberry-pi-for-block-building-on-the-cheap/

Chapter 9: Getting Creative With Your Pi 2

The best thing about the Raspberry Pi is its invitation for creativity. The microcomputer makes a great experience for those who are naturally curious and love to explore and create. With a little bit of inspiration, you can be using your Raspberry Pi 2 to tap into your imagination and awaken your creativity. Here a few projects that might pique your interest and get your creative juices flowing. Some of the projects feature the first generation Raspberry Pi, but do not worry, as they can all be created with the Pi 2 as well.

Color My Desk

This is a string of lights that will light up your office space and are publicly controllable. It is for the office worker who does not have much options in terms of customizing space, but still wants to have some control over the ambiance of their work environment. It is built on the Raspberry Pi and can be made to work with RGB lights and a web server. Learn more about this project at http://willmakesthings.com/color-my-desk/ and maybe you can take a minute to change the color of the project creator's desk on a day of your choosing. Just head over to http://colormydesk.com/

LED Display Machine

One Pi user has created a scrolling LED matrix that is powered by the Raspberry Pi. He has been able to use it to display new from ESPN's API on a quarter hourly basis, display news, and as a clock. He will also be programming it to be used in his upcoming wedding to organize seating. Guests will be able to scan their table cards, and the display will show their table number. Find out how to create this yourself at http://www.fuerstjh.com/projects/pi.html

CheckinDJ

This project uses near field communication enabled objects which are linked to the social network accounts of venue patrons in order to make a music play list that is based on the tastes of the customers present at any given time. This is an updated version of "The Jukebox" and is a truly creative use for the Raspberry Pi device. Check it out at http://www.checkindj.com/v2/

H2O IQ

Certainly one of the most creative things that can be done with your Pi 2, this project shows you how to design a device to be placed in your garden beside your plants. It runs on solar power and has a moisture sensor, is connected to a drip irrigation system and runs XBee. The Pi is able to read the moisture levels in the soil, and it is also a web server, which means that you can remotely look at the status of your plants and compare this to their ideal moisture level. You an also set up various water options and send them to the Pi, which will then relay the message to the drip system. For more about this awesome Pi project, visit http://blog.valkyriesavage.com/blog/2013/01/18/h2o-iq/

Chapter 10: Top Success Tips When Working with a Pi 2

Of course, in order to get the most out of your Pi 2, you have to know all of the ins and outs of using it successfully. There are a few things that you can do in order to avoid mistakes, and in turn, having a negative experience with your Pi. Here are a few tips that will ensure your success as you begin and continue your Raspberry Pi 2 journey.

Tip #1: Know the Limitations of Your Raspberry Pi 2

While there are many amazing things that the Pi 2 can do, which the Pi cannot, there are some things that the Pi 2 will not be able to do. It will benefit you to double check the needed items and software for any projects that you would like to take on, in which the user explicitly states that they used the first generation Raspberry Pi. Most projects are compatible with the Pi 2, thanks to it also being run with an ARM Processor, and most popular operating systems having been updated to function with the Pi.

In addition, blogs about the Pi will have likely been updated in order to reflect a version of the project that can be completed using the most recent version of the Pi. However, if you do not see any such updates, be sure to double check everything, or you will find that you are not able to complete your project to your satisfaction, which will lead to frustration and a marring of your overall Pi 2 experience.

Tip #2: Use the Right Power Source

Just like the Raspberry Pi, the Raspberry Pi 2 is powered using a 5V microUSB cord. The developers of the Pi and Pi2 chose this kind of cable for the power supply due to its global popularity. It is used to power all Android phones, most Blackberry devices, and is the standard power supply cable in Europe.

This is a great choice on the part of the developers, but it can become an issue when users think that they can use any old microUSB cable that they have lying around to power their Pi 2. This is not the case. Using an inadequate cable to power you Raspberry Pi 2 will cause it to malfunction. Things that can go wrong include the keyboard and mouse not working properly. It is important for you to check with your local electronics store if you are unsure about what kind of microUSB cable you have before setting up your Pi 2 in order to avoid any problems with the system's operation.

Tip #3: Handle Your Raspberry Pi 2 with Care

The Raspberry Pi 2 does not come with its board protected by a case, like most computers do. This means that you will have to either create a case for it, or buy one. In the meantime, you should be sure to handle it very carefully so as not to cause damage. Just like any computer, the Pi 2 is sensitive to static, repeated dropping and scratching. In order to keep your Raspberry Pi 2 free from harm, be sure to handle it with clean hands in a clean area after removing any jewelry. Also, be careful not to wear fabrics that can attract static when handling your Pi 2.

Chapter 11: Raspberry Pi Events, Communities and Meet Ups

One of the greatest things about the age of technology is the ability to become a part of a global community in order to share your passion for something, or learn new things. This is possible for Raspberry Pi users, especially, and it will certainly enhance your Raspberry Pi experience to keep abreast of Pi related events, forums and meet ups. Here are a few Pi community links that will likely be of interest.

Raspberry Jam

Raspberry Jams are organized by Raspberry Pi users in order to share knowledge about the Pi and meet other Pi enthusiasts. Attending a Raspberry Jam is an engaging way to learn more about the Raspberry Pi and what you can do with it. You will also be able to meet others who are as passionate about this device as you are. You can find a map with Raspberry Jam locations, to find out if there will be any in your area. There is also a calendar that lists upcoming events. You can find these resources at http://www.raspberrypi.org/jam/ If there are no upcoming events near you, you can run your own Jam, as anyone is allowed to.

All you have to do is find a place ,set a date and time and you will be able to attract Raspberry Pi enthusiasts in your area. There is a detailed list of guidelines for running your own Jam at http://www.raspberrpi.org/jam/how/ . It addresses frequently asked questions about things such as venue and sponsoring, as well as organizing talks and ticket prices. You can also read about featured Jams if you are contemplating attending one and would like to see what it will be like and add your Jam to the website database, once it has been organized.

Raspberry Pi Forums

If you have questions about your Pi, or would like to learn about the challenges some other members of the Pi community have faced, in order to arm yourself with knowledge, you can check out one of the several Raspberry Pi forums online. The Raspberry Pi Foundation website hosts several, covering topics such as troubleshooting, beginners tips and interesting projects. Members of the Pi community share their ideas and insights for your benefit, and once you have mastered your Pi, you may feel comfortable doing the same.

You can also engage in forums hosted on other sites, such as XDA forums. They have a discussion dedicated to Raspberry Pi hacking and development. You can also check out eLinux.org which has a wiki page about the Pi, and OpenELEC media center for information about several Raspberry Pi based discussions. Here are some links to a few websites to get you started as a member of the Raspberry Pi online community:

http://www.raspberrypi.org/forums/

http://elinux.org/RPi_Hub

http://openelec.tv/forum/124-raspberry-pi

http://forum.xda-developers.com/hardware-hacking/raspberry-pi

Raspberry Pi Meetups

To learn about other Raspberry Pi Meetups, you can go to meetup.com and check out some of the many Raspberry Pi related meetup groups. If you weren't able to find anything in your area on the Raspberry Pi Foundation Website, this site is your best bet. There are 242 groups in 172 cities all over the world that will be meeting up to discuss the Raspberry Pi, among other topics, according to the website. To see for yourself, go to http://raspberry-pi.meetup.com/

Chapter 12: Fantastic Online Resources for the Raspberry Pi

As evidenced by the many links presented to you thus far, there is quite a wealth of information about the Raspberry Pi to be found online. This chapter will give you a few extra resources to get you started and beyond, with your Raspberry Pi device.

Web Resources and Blogs

For educational use of the Raspberry Pi, one of the best places to find resources is the Raspberry Pi Foundation website. They feature links to resources for teaching and learning using the Raspberry Pi, as well as classroom friendly projects. Go to http://www.raspberypi.org/resources/

The MagPi is a downloadable free magazine, dedicated to being a resource for Raspberry Pi fans. You can download the latest issue at http://www.raspberrypi.org/magpi/ and you can also purchase it in print form if you would prefer to own a hard copy.

Reddit, home of one of the most extensive online communities, is a great place to find news about the Raspberry Pi, as well as great project ideas. You will find links to YouTube videos and instructables, and if you get stuck you will certainly be able to find someone with answers. www.reddit.com/r/raspberry_pi

On MakeUseOf, you can find articles on a wide range of topics related to the PI. You will be able to learn about making retro gaming centers, cloud storage devices, and much much more using your Raspberry Pi. You will also be able to find tutorials about how to make attractive custom cases to house your Pi. There is even a step by step guide to getting started with the Raspberry PI.

http://www.makeuseof.com/tag/raspberry-pi-creditcard-sized-arm-computer-25/

You should also take a look at blogs about the Raspberry Pi, of which there are many to choose from. One notable blog is on Adafruit.com. Here you can find all of the latest updates about the Raspberry Pi, as well as a few interesting projects for your databases. https://blog.adafruit.com/category/raspberry-pi/

Lifehacker, a notable blog site on a variety of topics, has a dedicated Raspberry Pi section, which will certainly be of interest to you. This is also a great place to check for emerging projects being done with the Pi, that you might like to try yourself. http://lifehacker.com/tag/raspberry-pi

Raspberry Pi Kid is a blog run by a thirteen year old. The epitome of the Raspberry Pi Foundation's aims, this kid talks about everything having to do with the Pi, from new developments, to failed experiments. Find this blog at
https://raspberrypikid.wordpress.com/

Print Resources

If you are interested in offline resources, there are some very useful books and magazines available about the Raspberry Pi.

Raspberry Pi User Guide by Eben Upton and Gareth Halfacre is co-written by one of the co-creators of the Raspberry PI, so you can imagine all of the great and valid information there is to be found in this book.

Haynes Raspberry Pi Manual takes a look at hardware, software, and projects that can be done using the Raspberry Pi. It is authored by Dr. Gray Girling, a Broadcom engineer who was closely involved in the Pi's development.

You might also want to take a look at *Programming the Raspberry Pi: Getting Started with Python*, a book that will five you all of the tools you need to learn Python and become a Raspberry PI programing master. This book will teach you how to use the Pi's GPIO port to interface with external devices and complete exciting projects, like building an LED clock.

Conclusion

Thank you again for downloading this book!

Hopefully, this book will be able to help you to get started on the journey towards using and truly enjoying your Raspberry Pi 2.

The Pi 2 is a great tool for teaching and learning programming and coding, as well as the fundamentals of computer science. You can create tons of fantastic things using the Raspberry Pi 2, and you can either do this by following the tutorials of others, or using your own imagination in order to make a creative invention of your own. Whatever you decide to do, make sure you follow the tips given in order to have success while working with your Pi 2.

This version of the Raspberry Pi is the most powerful and fastest yet. You will be able to use many kinds of operating systems, and programming languages as you continue on your Raspberry Pi journey.

With this amazing resource at your fingertips, you will be able to make the most of your Raspberry Pi 2 experience, starting today!

Printed in Great Britain
by Amazon.co.uk, Ltd.,
Marston Gate.